Myths and Legends About Digital Transformation.
What Success Looks Like.

Marc Israel

Myths and Legends About Digital Transformation. What Success Looks Like.

Cover Picture by Andras Vas on Unsplash

ISBN: 9781080734221
Imprint: Independently published

You can reach the author at marc.israel@aetheis.com

Myths and Legends About Digital Transformation.
What Success Looks Like.

Marc Israel
Founder, CEO, Author, Speaker

Table of content

Introduction

Digital Transformation has been in almost every business discussion for the last ten years. Digital technologies and startups have profoundly transformed business across the world. Industries have been changed forever. Uber is worth more than General Motors, AirBnB than Marriott, Kodak and Lego almost went bankrupt, just to name a few.

On the other side of the coin, the press is full of digital transformation failures, costing millions without getting the expected results. What did fail? What makes a digital transformation project different from other projects? Should it be IT-led? Some are the questions that this course will answer.

It brings close to 10 years of experience of its author into a pragmatic approach to Digital Transformation, applicable to any industry. Digital transformation, as you are going to see, is a business transformation, led from the top, that results in radical changes in how business is carried. It's also a long-term commitment to enabling a digital culture into the organization, learning from the startup world and adapting its reality to the organizations.

Above all, digital transformation is a journey, driven by people for people. If the adjective digital implies technology is present and is an important component, it's a means to an end, not the end. Technology is almost irrelevant. Almost because most of the technologies we will discuss are now mainstream and quasi-commodities. Digital transformation is a cultural change, one that benefits the employees, the processes, the organization, and first and foremost, the customers.

Buckle up, the ride is fast, bumpy, and exhilarating.

If you have any comments on the content of this manual, please send them to info@aetheis.com. Have a great read!

Notes

Objectives

- Understand the myths, legends and reality of digital transformation
- Have a holistic view of your business to define where to apply digital
- Take two steps back to see the big picture of your digital transformation
- Put your company on the right digital track
- Have a deep understanding of where to apply digital transformation
- Get out with ideas, strategies and tactics to apply digital transformation
- Be able to predict your future

Notes

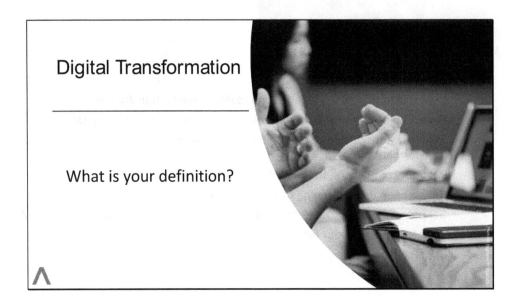

Provide your own definition of Digital Transformation. What it means to you, what it entails?

_____

Notes

Digital Transformation
What it is NOT

- Migration to cloud
- Update legacy
- Provide mobile email
- Implement instant messaging
- Hire tech gurus
- Trust IT vendors…

Notes

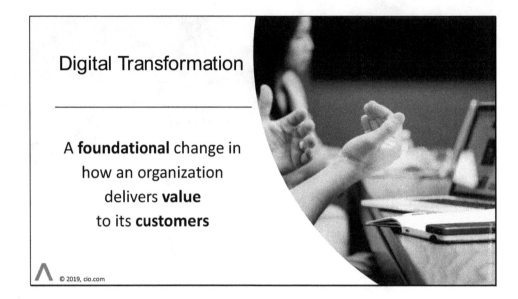

Note the 3 words in boldface:

- Foundational. Digital Transformation shakes the foundation of the organization. It goes deep into its roots.
- Value. Digital Transformation is not about doing things differently or faster, it's about doing them better to add value to the organization unique selling proposition.
- Customers. If it's not for customers, Digital Transformation is irrelevant. How to serve better our customers should be the central them of any digital transformation project.

Notes

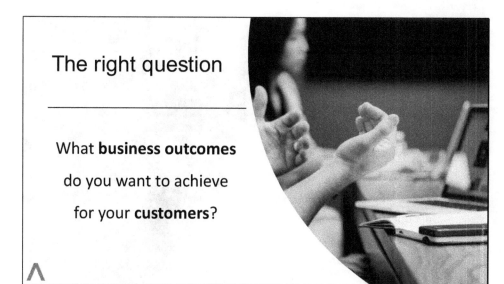

Notes

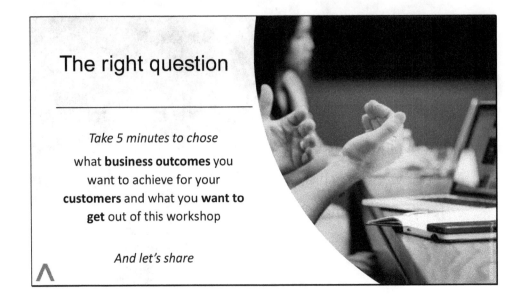

Note below what you would like to achieve with your digital transformation project, and what you want to get out of this workshop. Then let's share with each other.

___

Notes

Agenda

Digital Transformation, What It Is. Really!
- Internal Digital Transformation
- External Digital Transformation
- Edge Digital Transformation

Digital Transformation, Myths and Legends
- The Fat Startup
- The Thin Corporation
- Everything Digital

 Case Study

What does DT Success look like?
- Internal Success
- External Success
- Edge Success
- The Digitally Transformed Organization

The Lean and Agile Organization
- Digital Innovation Framework
- The Digital Board
- Fail Fast Forward

Notes

Agenda

Digital Transformation, What It Is. Really!
- Internal Digital Transformation
- External Digital Transformation
- Edge Digital Transformation

Digital Transformation, Myths and Legends
- The Fat Startup
- The Thin Corporation
- Everything Digital

 Case Study

What does DT Success look like?
- Internal Success
- External Success
- Edge Success
- The Digitally Transformed Organization

The Lean and Agile Organization
- Digital Innovation Framework
- The Digital Board
- Fail Fast Forward

Digital Transformation. What it is. Really!

___

Notes

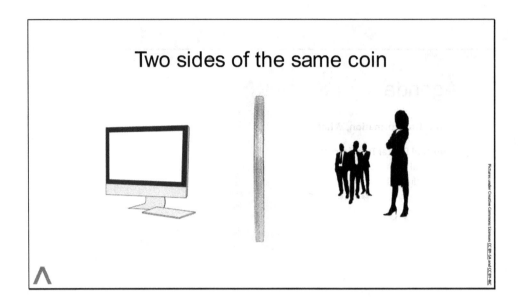

Digital transformation is about technology and people. The purpose of a car is to carry people and goods from one point to the other. We can glorify the technology that is used into the car, its design and raw products. However, the ultimate measures of success is how fast, how secure and how comfortable is the car. The same applies to digital transformation. People without technology or technology without people are only half the job done.

Notes

First myth we are meeting in the course. Because of the adjective digital, we tend to think that digital transformation is all about technology. But technology is a means to an end: delivering more value to our customers. Some traditional businesses are digitally transformed with very basic technology. Technology does not make digital transformation, It's a big mistake to consider digital transformation only through the technology lens. It's a pure recipe for failure!

Notes

Digital Transformation starts from the inside, at each employee level. It may drive productivity enhancements; however, it's focused on new methods of working to serve customers better.

- Working methods: What is between the employees and the customers that could be improved, changed, or suppressed? Who can/should work remotely? How can you improve customers touch points?
- Management methods: Do you measure employee engagement, impact and effectiveness? How do you employee's job to customers? What is employee measure of success?
- Communication methods: Do you use/encourage modern communication methods, like instance messaging, in a secure way? What are your mobile policies?
- Collaboration methods: Do you still rely on physical meetings or online can work? Are you sharing documents easily and seamlessly, inside and outside your company? Is collaboration transparent?
- IT Control: Centralized or decentralized control? Cloud or not cloud? Shadow IT?

Notes

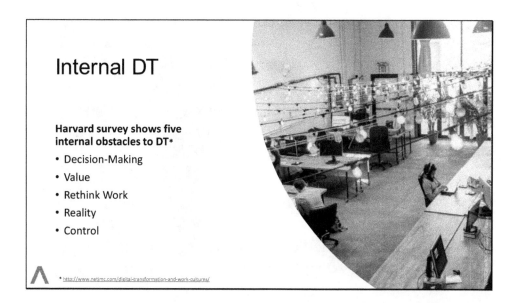

"**Slow or stalled decision-making** caused by internal politics, competing priorities, or attempting to reach consensus.

Inability to prove business value of digital through traditional ROI calculations, resulting in lack of senior management sponsorship.

Too much focus on technology rather than willingness to address deep change and rethink how people work.

Lack of understanding operational issues at the decision-making level and difficulties when going from theory to practice.

Fear of losing control by management or central functions, and fears that employees will waste time on social platforms."

https://hbr.org/2015/08/the-company-cultures-that-help-or-hinder-digital-transformation

Notes

External DT

- Customer experience is everyone's job
- Customer feedback is critical
- Automation needs to add value not only lower cost and save time
- Data Driven Evolution

Digital transformation should be focused on customer experience. Do you know and have experienced your customer's journey? Which data points are you gathering? If automation leads to job losses, there's something wrong in the way you implement/chose the technology! External digital transformation is about value creation, exclusively!

Notes

Here are a few questions to ask about your customer experience. One way to start rethinking your customer experience and journey is to list all your customer touch points: are they congruent? Is customer experience consistent? Can you measure it?

Notes

What I call edge digital transformation is all those processes and operations that may not seem correlated to customer engagement: supply chain, manufacturing, product creation, business model assumptions. A digital transformation project is an ideal candidate to challenge assumptions and rethink the way you work ... deeply! Map out what is the product journey from thinking about new product creation to servicing it once sold, then look at how you can improve each step.

Notes

Let's look at three case studies to understand how processes, operations and business models play a critical role in digital transformation:

- Marriott & AirBnB. Marriott could have invented AirBnB but was, and still is, stuck in the classical hospitality paradigm. How and why AirBnB challenged the hospitality market and became more valuable than Marriott is less than 10 years?

- Dollar Shave Club is less known in EMEA. It's a subscription-based model to get razor blades delivered directly to avoid missing them and getting the best quality at the best price. Launched in 2010, Dollar Shave Club raised around 100M USD from 2012 until 2015. reported 3.2 million subscribers, launched last year in the UK. On July 19, 2016, Dollar Shave Club was acquired by Unilever for a reported $1 billion in cash. What did they do differently?

- Amazon is the global giant that is fast killing retail physical shopping, What is their secret sauce and what can we learn from it?

Notes

Agenda

Digital Transformation, What It Is. Really!
- Internal Digital Transformation
- External Digital Transformation
- Edge Digital Transformation

Digital Transformation, Myths and Legends
- The Fat Startup
- The Thin Corporation
- Everything Digital

Case Study

What does DT Success look like?
- Internal Success
- External Success
- Edge Success
- The Digitally Transformed Organization

The Lean and Agile Organization
- Digital Innovation Framework
- The Digital Board
- Fail Fast Forward

Digital Transformation. Myths and Legends

Notes

Second myth: digital transformation is a big organization problem. As a small or medium organization, I'm not concerned. My customers work with us because they all know us, have deep personal relationship and know the value we are providing. Unfortunately, if this is true on the outside, it may lead to a myopic view of your business. All customers are looking for the best value for money and will challenge the relationship if it does not provide the best value.

Notes

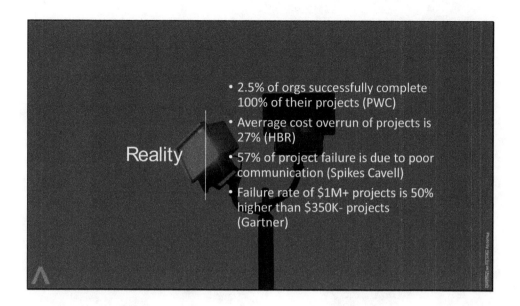

Here are a few interesting numbers that need to be kept in mind when embarking on any project, and even more particularly a digital transformation project.

Notes

Nouvelle Cuisine syndrome is about getting the hype of new things without knowing the good old recipes. Startup success hides three tangible truths:

1. A startup is very thin -> Instagram had 13 employees when it was purchased US$1B by Facebook.
2. A startup is mission driven -> Google: Information, organized!
3. Technology is an enabler -> mobile is central but the underlying technology, beyond being a cloud-based, is irrelevant. Whether IBM, Microsoft, Oracle, Amazon or smaller vendors, any technology will allow the mission to be achieved.

Willing to apply a startup mentality does not start with technology at all!

Notes

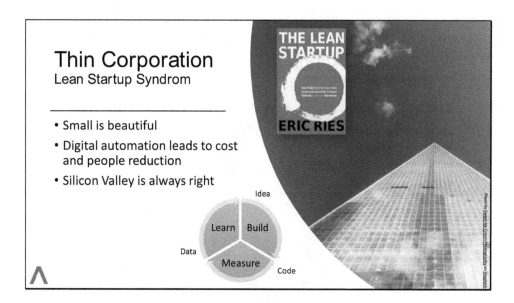

Avoiding the fat startup approach sometimes leads to go too thin. There are some truths in the lean startup model that needs to fit in the organization culture, particularly the lean startup model described by Eric Ries in the bestseller The Lean Startup:

- Build the idea
- Measure the results
- Learn from the whole process and repeat

Doing this obfuscates the fact that the biggest challenge to tackle sits with people, culture and adoption. It's at the core of any startup as well: users!

Notes

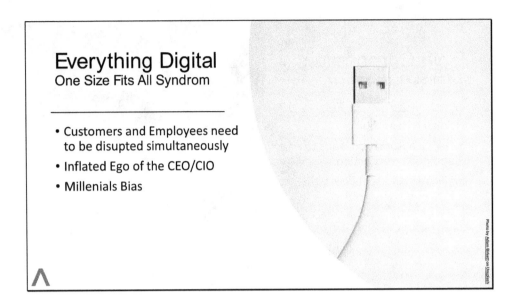

Think about the time it took you to adopt any new technology or behavior. It takes months if not years to instill change. Change is hard, change is messy, change is uncomfortable. If the employees and not comfortable, they will make your customers uncomfortable, and vice versa.

Two key aspects of the everything digital approach can make the digital transformation project fail:

- The inflated ego of the CEO/COO who wants to lead fast chance despite wrong signals coming either from employees or customers. The Orange suicidal rate some years ago was clearly ignored and cost Orange some leadership position.
- The millennial bias and the one that goes with it, senior inadaptability to new digital technology. It's the customer who matters. If you are serving millennials, then your culture needs to be millennial focused, however, depending on your customer personas you may need to reconsider the digital approach.

Notes

Third myth: digital transformation will kill some jobs and will have a reducing effect on the workforce. This may happen, in the mid or longer term, but that may also not happen. Digital transformation will have a deep effect on working, management, communication and collaboration methods. Some employees may be forced to change jobs; however, this needs to be evaluated in the overall implementation plan. 67% of organization have created positions due to a Digital Transformation project or stayed flat (Futurum, 2018)

Notes

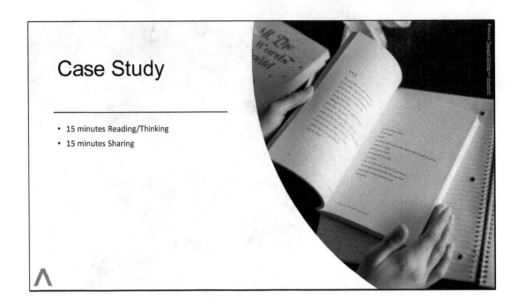

Case Study

Notes

Agenda

Digital Transformation, What It Is. Really!
* Internal Digital Transformation
* External Digital Transformation
* Edge Digital Transformation

Digital Transformation, Myths and Legends
* The Fat Startup
* The Thin Corporation
* Everything Digital

 Case Study

What does DT Success look like?
* Internal Success
* External Success
* Edge Success
* **The** Digitally Transformed Organization

The Lean and Agile Organization
* Digital Innovation Framework
* The Digital Board
* Fail Fast Forward

What does DT Success Look Like?

Notes

Digital Transformation should come from the top and have the total buy-in both from the executive committee and the board of directors. If your digital transformation project does not start from the top, you will need to get the buy-in before starting and ensure at least one executive is leading the effort.

Notes

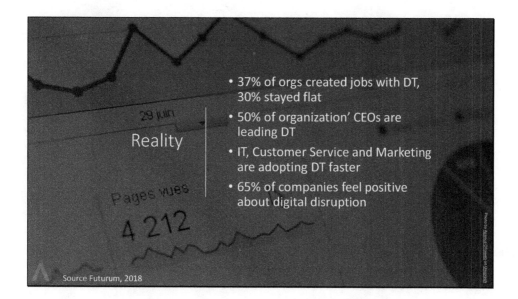

Another set of interesting positive statistics when it comes to digital transformation.

Notes

An interesting paper about digitization of the workplace: The Digital Workplace is Key to Digital Innovation, MIT Sloan Center for Information Systems Research, Dery, Sebastian and van der Meuylen, June 2017 (16:2) | MIS Quarterly Executive, University of Minnesota.

Adoption should be your primary goal, not the deployment of any new technology. To drive adoption, here are 5 key success factors, not in any particular priority order:

- **Lead from the top**. We talked a lot about this. The CEO/COO should over communicate and enlist champions to lead the change.
- **Engage at every level**. No employees left behind. What's in it for everybody in the change?
- **Choose the right technology**. If the foundational technology is somehow irrelevant, the adoption of its features is critical and needs to be aligned to the new methodologies. Ease of use and adoption should come first, without discounting the training needs.
- **Find your purpose**. Why are you doing what you are doing? Be clear and ensure employees buy-in.
- **Change management is not an option**. We know change is hard. Change should be managed. Relying on automatic adoption because the technology makes sense or is easy to use is a guarantee for failure.

Notes

External digital transformation is all about changing, improving, or enhancing the customer experience. Success factors are focused around it.

- Focus on customer experience and measure it. Measure, whether quantitative or qualitative are central to the enhancement of the experience. Know your customer journey, map it and discover all the potential KPIs. Can you think of some?
- Be surgical by making incremental changes. Big Bangs don't yield the same results as small incremental changes that compound over time.
- Find and communicate around your why. Why you are doing what you are doing.
- Focus on data quality. Think of all the touch points a customer has. Capture, clean and measure on a constant basis.

Notes

Beyond enabling new business models, succeeding in transforming the edge lies into three dimensions:

- Productivity. Producing more with the same or improved quality.
- Connectivity. Gathering more qualitative data to derive meaningful information.
- Standardization. Seeking adherence to norms and standards. Not a clear differentiator but a way to guarantee quality of the processes and procedures. When norms or standards do not exist, participate in their creation.

Notes

Myth number 4. Digital transformation ends when technology is deployed and adopted. Well, Digital Transformation knows no end. Once a project is over, another one has already started. Digital innovation should be part of the organization culture to always drive forward constant change.

Notes

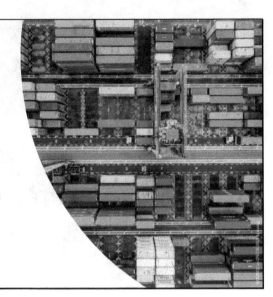

What does a digitally transform organization look like? Here are a few principles to adapt:

- **The lean startup model**. Each project should define a minimum viable outcome/product and work towards it. Once attained, measure, learn and expand.
- **Organization change pace**. Be on the lookout to new technologies. Have an innovation team constantly testing new technologies and business models. Be your own disruptor.
- **Innovation at the heart**. Innovation needs to be on the CEO's agenda at every meeting. A culture of constant innovation guarantees not to miss opportunities.

Notes

Agenda

Digital Transformation, What It Is. Really!
* Internal Digital Transformation
* External Digital Transformation
* Edge Digital Transformation

Digital Transformation, Myths and Legends
* The Fat Startup
* The Thin Corporation
* Everything Digital

 Case Study

What does DT Success look like?
* Internal Success
* External Success
* Edge Success
* The Digitally Transformed Organization

The Lean and Agile Organization
* Digital Innovation Framework
* The Digital Board
* Fail Fast Forward

The Lean and Agile Organization

Notes

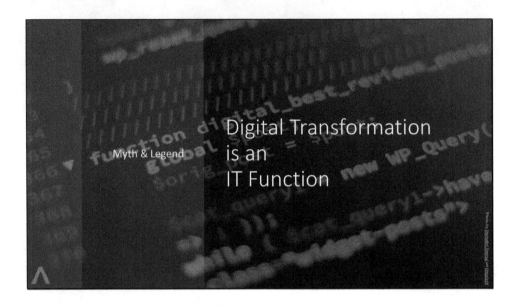

Fifth and final myth. Digital transformation is an IT function. Not only it is not, but it should not be! Digital transformation is a business and people process, not an IT one. IT comes as the support, not the driver!

Notes

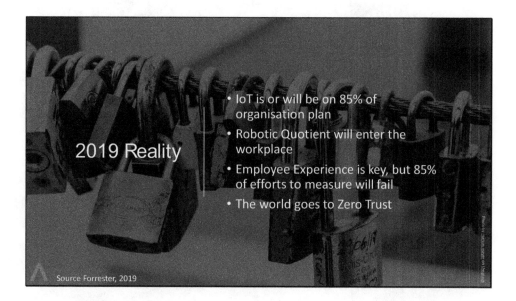

Some new realities in 2019 based on Forrester predictions.

Notes

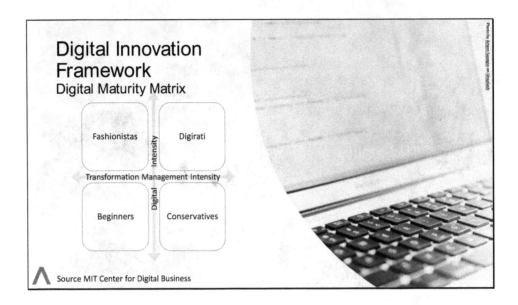

Beginners = Skepticism about digital, immature digital culture, may carry some experiments.

Fashionistas = Pockets of advanced digital technologies (social, mobile…), no vision, lack of coordination, digital culture in silos.

Conservatives = underdeveloped digital vision, digital culture in the making, leveraging mature digital technologies (web, mobile).

Digirati = Strong digital vision, good governance, digital initiatives generating value, strong digital culture.

Notes

Whatever the size of your company or the anticipated magnitude of your digital transformation project, here's a simple framework to consider.

1. Start articulating your digital vision and strategy. How do you see your organization in 10 or 15 years from now? What drives it? What are the key values you want to build on?
2. How do you see your different business units align around this vision? How can you tie vision and business together? This step is critical as part of your success lies in articulating perfectly business and technology.
3. How does the digital governance will be organized? Who owns what? Ensure lead is coming from the top.
4. What are the actions you are or will be taking to ensure people engagement and the development of a digital customer?
5. What are your current digital capabilities and the ones you will need to acquire? How will you acquire them? Are your current training programs aligned with your digital strategy? If not, how to align them?
6. What competitive advantage will you derive from digital transformation? This should be clearly stated in our unique selling proposition.

Notes

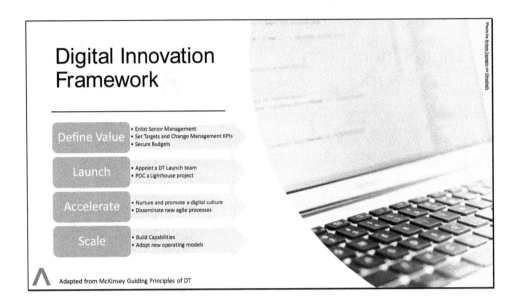

Once you've described the previous points, it's time to plan and move to execution.

1. **Define value**. Your strategy set, ensure the CEO or somebody he/she will appoint acts as the executive sponsor for the project and takes his/her role at heart. Define with him/her the KPIs for this project and follow his guidance to secure budgets. An easy mistake is to under budget, particularly on the change management side. Change is always hard and messy!

2. **Launch**. The lean startup model encourages you to define the minimum viable product. Work towards it. This will become your proof-of-concept. The idea of a throwable PoC is ridiculous. A PoC should be the first iteration of your creative endeavor. It allows you to test the concept, enlist the first users and correct course before it becomes too costly to fail.

3. **Accelerate**. Start disseminating the results of the POC and use the learning to adapt the next cycle of release. Work with the sponsor to adapt the existing process to the new reality until adopted by the entire organization.

4. **Scale**. This is the ultimate step. Leverage all the learning to the next projects, make the lean methodology, the default choice and build the necessary capabilities for the n+1 project.

Notes

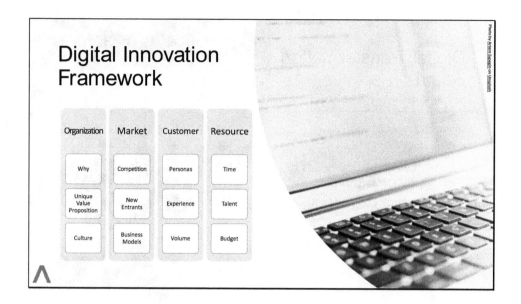

During your strategy definition and tactical execution, use the following four dimensions to articulate each element and step:

- **Organization**. What is your why, your unique value proposition to your customers and employees, and your own culture?
- **Market**. Who are your competitors, the new ones, their business model? How is this fitting with yours?
- **Customers**. How many do you have? How do you intend to grow? Define your personas and unique experience.
- **Resources**. Time, talent and budget. Do they all fit within your project?

Notes

Better than a steering committee, make a DT board. Have one board of directors member sitting on it, but not somebody picked at random. He/she should be a digital transformer, a person who has already gone through the journey of transforming a traditional business digitally. He/she may not be the most senior leader in terms of general management but should be the most digitally astute.
Implicating the board of directors in the DT project is an opportunity to create a digital boardroom.

https://hbr.org/2017/07/the-board-directors-you-need-for-a-digital-transformation

Notes

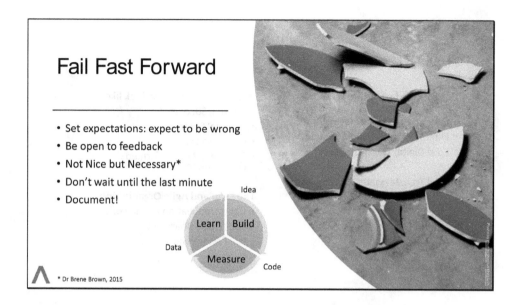

The notion of failing fast has always been one attributed to startups. However, failing forward seems better, meaning, learning from the failure and continue moving on. The best way to fail fast forward graciously is by following those advices:

- **Be super open to feedback**. It's not against you, it's for the business! Ensure to separate business criticism from personal ones.
- **Failing is not nice, it's necessary**. You don't learn to ride a bike by reading how to ride one. You need to try and fall!
- **Set expectations right**. What will you learn if you fail? What will the situation look like if you fail?
- **Communicate early and frequently**. The sooner, the better as we say.
- **Document everything**. Apply technology to document everything. You can follow Bridgewater examples who records every meeting and make recordings available to every employee!

Here are two interesting articles about failing forward. https://www.advantexe.com/blog/3-tips-for-leading-a-business-environment-to-really-fail-fast-forward, https://www.huffpost.com/entry/fail-forward-fast-get-ove_b_4555393

Notes

Agenda

Digital Transformation, What It Is. Really!
- Internal Digital Transformation
- External Digital Transformation
- Edge Digital Transformation

Digital Transformation, Myths and Legends
- The Fat Startup
- The Thin Corporation
- Everything Digital

Case Study

What does DT Success look like?
- Internal Success
- External Success
- Edge Success
- The Digitally Transformed Organization

The Lean and Agile Organization
- Digital Innovation Framework
- The Digital Board
- Fail Fast Forward

Notes

Conclusion

We are that the end of this fast-paced course, but only at the beginning of your transformation. Here are the key elements to build your DT on:

- Digital Transformation is a **foundational** change in how an organization delivers **value** to its **customers**. It's not about IT, technology or hype. It's about changing the organization for the good of its customers.
- Envision the digital future of your organization. How will your organization be in 10 to 15 years from now? Can you describe it in vivid terms?
- The lean startup model applied to DT. Build a minimum viable product, measure, learn, repeat.
- Lead the change from the top. Without executive sponsorship, you will not be successful. Ensure the change is led, embraced and embodied from the top management.

I wish you a great digital transformation!

Marc Israel

_____

Notes

Going Further

- David Rogers, The Digital Transformation Playbook: Rethink Your Business for the Digital Age, 2016, Columbia Business School Publishing

- Eric Ries, The Lean Startup: How Today's Entrepreneurs Use Continuous Innovation to Create Radically Successful Businesses, 2011, Currency

- Gerald Kane, The Technology Fallacy: How People Are the Real Key to Digital Transformation, 2019, MIT Press

- Jeff Dyer, Innovation Capital: How to Compete--and Win--Like the World's Most Innovative Leaders, 2019, HBR Press

- John Rosman, Think Like Amazon: 50 1/2 Ideas to Become a Digital Leader, 2019, McGraw-Hill Education

- Michael Cusumano, The Business of Platforms: Strategy in the Age of Digital Competition, Innovation, and Power, 2019, HarperBusiness

- Nicolaj Siggelkow, Connected Strategy: Building Continuous Customer Relationships for Competitive Advantage, 2018, HBR Press

- Tom Siebel, Digital Transformation: Survive and Thrive in an Era of Mass Extinction, 2019, RosettaBooks

Notes

Thank you!

Notes

Myths and Legends About Digital Transformation. What Success Looks Like.